Halloween

Why We Celebrate It the Way We Do

by Martin Hintz and Kate Hintz

CAPSTONE PRESS

MANKATO

C A P S T O N E   P R E S S

818 North Willow Street • Mankato, MN 56001

Library of Congress Cataloging-in-Publication Data
Hintz, Martin
   Halloween : why we celebrate it the way we do / by
   Martin and Kate Hintz.
   p. cm. -- (Celebrate series)
   Includes bibliographical references and index.
   Summary: Describes the origins of some of the customs
   and traditions connected with Halloween and describes
   various ways to celebrate this holiday.
   ISBN 1-56065-326-4 (hc)
   ISBN 0-7368-8081-X (pb)
   1. Halloween--Juvenile literature. [1. Halloween.]
I. Hintz, Kate. II. Title. III. Series.
GT4965.H55   1996
394.2'646--dc20   95-45616
                                              CIP
                                               AC

Photo credits

Bob Firth: pp. 1, 24, 30, 42.
Paula Borchardt: cover, pp. 6-7.
Archive Photos: pp. 10, 14, 16, 19, 29, 32, 47.
Peter Ford: pp. 20-21, 34, 40.
Visuals Unlimited/Hank Andrews: pp. 23, 26, 37.

Table of Contents

Chapter 1 Celebrate Halloween 5

Chapter 2 The History of Halloween 11

Chapter 3 Halloween Symbols.........................15

Chapter 4 Trick or Treat..................................27

Chapter 5 Get Ready for Halloween................33

Glossary...43

To Learn More 44

Useful Addresses..46

Index 48

Words in **boldface** type in the text are defined in the Glossary in the back of this book.

Chapter 1

Celebrate Halloween

Halloween is a time of fun. People decorate their homes with orange and black. Some people hang up cardboard witches and cats. Pumpkins are carved into jack-o'-lanterns. Candles light up their faces.

Children go trick-or-treating and bring home candy. People go to haunted houses to be scared.

Costume parties are great fun. Some people think for a whole year about what they will

A simple Halloween costume can also be scary.

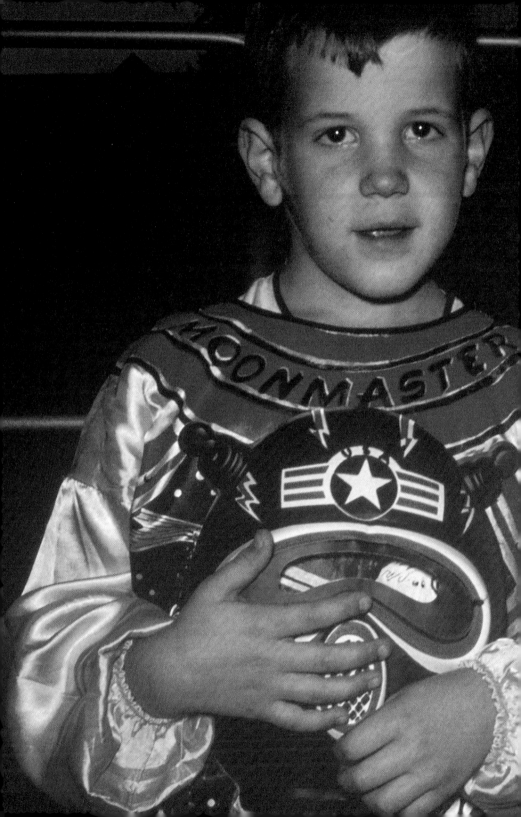

wear for Halloween. Some of the costumes are unusual. Some are scary. Some are funny. Often, prizes for the best costumes are awarded.

Trick or Treat

Children wear costumes to trick-or-treat. They knock on doors or ring doorbells. When the door opens, the young people yell, "Trick or Treat." Originally, if children did not get a treat, they would play a trick.

Most children do not play tricks anymore. Almost everyone has treats to give out. Those who do not want to give out treats turn their lights off. This tells trick-or-treaters not to go to that house.

Jack-o'-lanterns

Carving jack-o'-lanterns from pumpkins is fun, too. Some people want their jack-o'-lanterns to be friendly. Others want them to be scary. Many people give their jack-o'-lanterns jagged teeth. They often cut triangles for the eyes and nose.

Haunted Houses

Many groups and some families put on haunted houses. They decorate rooms or whole houses. They do it to scare people.

People in costumes jump out from closets. Moans, screams, and evil laughter are in the air. Tombstones decorate the yard.

A mad scientist's workshop can be a part of your Halloween fun. The workshop has all the parts of a fake monster, from his fake eyeballs to his fake toes. It can be gross, but it is fun, too.

Chapter 2

The History of Halloween

Halloween is one of the oldest holidays. It has been celebrated for thousands of years. Today, it is a time of fun. But long ago, people believed that witches, ghosts, and **goblins** were real.

The God of the Dead

The **Celts** lived in Europe more than 2,500 years ago. They worshipped nature. The sun was one of their gods.

Long ago, witches were thought of as evil, and they were persecuted.

Winter was a confusing time for the Celts. They did not understand why it was dark so much of the time. They made up stories to explain why the sun disappeared.

One of the stories said that the sun and Samhain fought a battle. Samhain was the god of the dead. The sun lost and was held prisoner during the winter.

The Celts believed that winter was the season of death. They thought that Samhain called the dead to walk the earth once a year. Some people believed the souls of the dead were picking out who would die that year.

Fire

Celtic priests were called Druids. The Celts believed the Druids had magical powers. The Druids had a **ceremony** in the fall to help the sun. They built huge fires. The fire was hot like the sun. They thought it would free the sun.

The Druids used the fire to frighten away the dead. They wore masks and costumes. The masks would scare the spirits. The costumes would keep the spirits from recognizing people. If the spirits could not recognize the people, they could not pick them to die.

Roman Festivals

The Romans invaded the Celtic lands about 2,000 years ago. They ruled the Celts for 400 years.

The Romans had two celebrations in the fall. One was a harvest festival. During this festival, friends gave each other apples. The other festival honored the dead. Eventually, the Roman holidays and the Celtic fire holiday became one large festival.

All Saints' Day

In 835, the Roman Catholic Church tried to change the holiday. The Church wanted a holiday of its own. Church leaders set aside All Saints' Day to honor their saints who had died.

This holy day was also called All Hallows' Day or Hallowmas. It was celebrated on November 1. The day before, October 31, was then known as All Hallows' Even. Eventually, it was called Halloween.

Chapter 3

Halloween Symbols

Certain things remind people of Halloween. Think of a witch or a ghost. Think of jack-o'-lanterns and magic. Think of black and orange. These are **symbols** of Halloween.

Black and Orange

Black and orange are everywhere at Halloween. Witches are usually dressed in black. Their cats are black. Pumpkins are orange.

In ancient times, the colors had meanings. Black stood for death and night. Orange stood

The witch, with her broomstick and black cat, has long been a symbol of Halloween.

for the harvest. Orange was also the color of the fire used to keep the demons away.

Witches

The witch has been a symbol of Halloween for a long time. Witches are often pictured with a broomstick and a black cat.

Long ago, people believed in witches who had magical powers. They thought witches could cast spells. Witches were not thought of as bad at first. But through the years, people

The most famous witch trials took place in Salem.

began to believe that witches were evil. They thought they could cause sickness, death, and bad weather. They thought witches could change into animals. People said that witches worshipped the devil.

Several times a year, witches would get together. They met in a sacred spot deep in the forest. This was called a witches' sabbat. One of the most important sabbats was on Halloween.

Many innocent people were killed when they were accused of being witches. There were even witch trials in early America. The most **infamous** stories about witches are from Salem, Massachusetts. Many innocent women were burned to death during the Salem Witch Trials in 1692.

There are witches today who get together for religious ceremonies. But they are no longer persecuted.

Cats and Broomsticks

People believed witches turned themselves into cats. They also believed cats had magical powers and could see in the dark. Because cats are quiet and independent, people thought they were spirits.

Many years ago, before there were many bridges, men often carried long poles. They used them to **vault** over ditches.

Sometimes women would use their broomsticks to jump over small streams. It looked like they were flying. This might be the reason people thought that witches flew around on broomsticks.

Pumpkins and Jack-o'-lanterns

Carving pumpkins into jack-o'-lanterns is a Halloween **tradition.** Jack-o'-lanterns have a candle inside that lights their faces. Some people hold pumpkin-carving contests. Many people put a jack-o'-lantern in a window or on the front step.

A **folk tale** explains where the jack-o'-lantern came from. It says there was once a man named Jack who tricked the devil. Jack

Carving pumpkins for jack-o'-lanterns is a Halloween tradition.

got the devil to promise not to take his soul. The devil was angry. When Jack died, the devil made his spirit roam the earth forever.

Jack complained to the devil that it was too dark. So the devil gave him a burning coal. Jack put the coal in a turnip because it was so hot. This was the first jack-o'-lantern.

It was not until the tradition came to North America that pumpkins were used for jack-o'-lanterns. Pumpkins were easier to carve than turnips.

Ghosts, Skeletons, and Graveyards

In ancient times, people were afraid of ghosts and skeletons. Any bad thing that happened was blamed on the spirits of the dead.

People believed that ghosts wandered the earth in search of food and warmth. To please them, people left out food and kept fires burning on Halloween. Hungry people ate the food. When they started taking the dishes with the food, the custom stopped.

In ancient times, the Druids dressed up to scare away evil spirits.

Graveyards were believed to be the home of ghosts. If you met a ghost in a graveyard, it was a warning of death. People believed that ghosts danced in the graveyard on Halloween. They thought that skeletons rattled their bones.

Everyone tries to be scary on Halloween.

Today, people dress up like ghosts and skeletons on Halloween. Yards are decorated with tombstones. It is all for fun.

Magic

Magic fits in with the mystery of Halloween. Harry Houdini was one of the most famous magicians of all time. He could escape from prisons. He could get out of handcuffs and locked suitcases, even when they were thrown into a lake. He did a trick that made it look like he could walk through walls.

Houdini died on Halloween in 1926. His death is observed by many magicians. October 31 is National Magic Day.

Costumes and Masks

Costumes and masks were once used to try to scare away ghosts and spirits. People thought that ugly masks would make the demons think the person wearing the mask was a demon, too. That way the demon would be scared of them.

People danced around a fire because they thought light and the color red chased away spirits.

Eventually, children dressed up as ghosts, witches, and demons to scare their neighbors. A few decades ago, children started playing tricks on their neighbors if they did not get a treat. This was the beginning of modern trick or treating.

Chapter 4

Trick or Treat

Trick or treating has a long history. It started with the Roman harvest festivals, when people gave apples to their friends. This started the tradition of giving and getting treats on Halloween.

Irish immigrants brought many of their favorite Halloween customs with them to North America in the 19th century. They played games and pranks. They also brought the idea of turnip jack-o'-lanterns.

Trick-or-treaters get ready for a night of candy collecting.

Halloween tricks became popular. People would find chairs in trees and wagons on top of barns. The people playing the tricks thought they were funny. But some of the tricks hurt people. That made Halloween less fun.

So the customs changed. People wanted Halloween to be a good time. Children stopped playing tricks, and most everyone gave out treats.

Trick-or-Treat for UNICEF

In 1950, a new Halloween custom began. Members of a youth group in Philadelphia collected money for poor children all around the world. When they went trick-or-treating, they carried empty milk cartons and asked for money. They collected $17.

The money was given to UNICEF, the United Nations International Children's Emergency Fund. UNICEF helps children all

Some children trick-or-treat for UNICEF and collect money for the poor children of the world.

over the world who are hungry, poor, or sick. Soon, many children were trick-or-treating for UNICEF.

U.S. President Lyndon Johnson officially recognized the trick-or-treat for UNICEF program in 1967. Today, children trick-or-treating for UNICEF carry special cartons.

Keeping Halloween Safe

Parents now tell their children to look over their treats. They should not eat anything that is not wrapped. Razor blades and needles have been stuck in unwrapped treats. Some treats have also been poisoned.

Children should trick or treat only in groups. They should go only to houses they know. They should be careful when crossing streets or running down sidewalks.

Costumes also should be safe. They should be fireproof. Make sure the costume is reflective or wear reflective tape. Children should be sure they do not trip over their costumes.

A mask is an important part of a Halloween costume.

Chapter 5

Get Ready for Halloween

You can do many things to prepare for Halloween. You can make your own costume and mask. You can carve a jack-o'-lantern. You can even create your own haunted house.

How to Make a Costume

Do you want to dress like a pirate? Tie a bandanna around your head. Put a sash around your waist. Wear old, torn clothes.

Jack-o'-lanterns can be funny, scary, or happy.

Then draw a sword on a long piece of cardboard. Cut it out carefully with scissors. Wrap it with aluminum foil. You can make an eye patch with black construction paper and a string.

Becoming a ghost is simple, too. Find an old sheet and cut eyeholes in it. Put the sheet over your head. Line up your eyes with the eyeholes. Moan loudly.

You can even become a scarecrow. For the head, crumple a brown paper bag. Cut out eyes

An air-filled jack-o'-lantern guards a pumpkin patch.

and a mouth. Cut strips from another paper bag for the hair. Glue them to the bag.

Wear your oldest clothes. Stuff straw or more paper strips into your sleeves and pant legs. The ends should stick out. Tie your sleeves and pant legs with string. This will keep the straw from falling out. Put on an old hat.

Use your imagination to think of other characters. Trick or treating is extra fun if you wear a costume you have made yourself.

How to Make a Mask

Masks can be made from paper bags. Use colored yarn for hair. Cut out funny eyes. Use crayons to draw silly designs on the mask.

Paper plates also make good masks. Cut out eyes, a mouth, and a place for your nose. Glue or tape a paper cup over the nose hole. Draw designs on your mask.

Poke two holes near the edges of the plate. Tie a string or ribbon through the holes. Put the mask on your face. Tie the string behind your head.

How to Carve a Pumpkin

Here is how to carve a pumpkin. First, draw the face you want on the pumpkin. Your jack-o'-lantern can be scary, happy, or goofy.

Use a knife to cut a hole around the stem of the pumpkin. Children should ask for help from an adult. Make the hole big enough to fit your hand inside. Scoop out the pulp and seeds with a heavy spoon. Carve out the eyes, nose, and mouth. When the inside is clean and the face carved, find a candle.

Light the candle and let some of the wax drip to the bottom of the pumpkin. Stick the bottom of your candle in the hot wax. The wax will get hard. The candle will stay there without falling over. Put your jack-o'-lantern where people walking by will see it. On a front porch or in a window is a good place.

Save the pumpkin seeds. Wash them and let them dry. Preheat the oven to 325 degrees. Lightly coat the seeds with melted butter or oil. Spinkle them with salt. Spread in a baking dish. Bake for 25 minutes or until the seeds are golden brown.

Use your imagination to think of costumes.

The Celts thought the dead came out on Halloween.

If you do not want to carve a pumpkin, you can paint a face on the outside. You can glue macaroni or seeds on it for a funny look.

How to Haunt Your House

You can make your home a spooky place. Invite your friends over for a party. Make invitations with black paper. Draw pictures of ghosts and monsters on them.

Make your house scary. Put black construction paper over the windows to make a room dark. Hang black threads from the ceiling. When the lights are out, the threads feel like cobwebs.

Cover the furniture with old sheets. A chair can look like a lumpy ghost. A red light bulb

Scary costumes and scary sounds add to Halloween's fun.

can make scary shadows. Make tombstones out of white cardboard. Set them around the room.

Make a tape of scary music. Rattle chains. Scream. Moan and laugh an evil laugh. Howl like a wolf. You can buy sound effects recordings at stores, or check with your local library. They might have a recording you can borrow.

Have your friends and family help you. They can dress in costumes and jump out of

Some farms grow hundreds of pumpkins just for Halloween.

closets or corners. Turn off the lights. In the dark, everything seems scarier.

How to Scare Your Friends

Set up a mad scientist's workshop to scare people. Make monster parts from food or other things around your house. You can trick your friends into thinking a handful of cooked spaghetti is a monster brain.

A bowl of peeled grapes feels like cold eyeballs. An old mop feels like witch hair. Put a piece of fur inside a shoe box. Say that it is your pet rat. Everybody will yell when they touch it.

Broken pretzels feel like teeth. Say that a bowl of Jell-O is monster guts. Cut up slimy hot dogs for toes. Maybe you can think of some more monster parts.

Have people touch your monster parts without being able to see them. Put the parts in boxes with holes in the tops. Keep the room dark.

How to Make Halloween Great

Most holidays have a serious side. Thanksgiving is for giving thanks. Christmas celebrates the birth of Jesus. The Fourth of July celebrates the beginning of a country.

But Halloween has no serious side. People celebrate it because it is fun. Have a great time. Tell ghost stories. Play games. Scare your friends. Scare yourself. Have fun.

Children have fun at Halloween.

Glossary

Celts—ancient European people

ceremony—formal act performed in honor or celebration of a special occasion

folk tale—a legend handed down by word of mouth

goblin—ugly, humanlike evil spirit

infamous—having a bad reputation

magician—entertainer who performs tricks

symbol—something that stands for another thing

tradition—customs, beliefs, and ceremonies handed down from generation to generation

vault—to jump over objects or ditches aided by a long pole

To Learn More

Barth, Edna. *Witches, Pumpkins, and Grinning Ghosts.* New York: The Seabury Press, 1972.

Corwin, Judith Hoffman. *Halloween Fun.* New York: Julian Messner, 1983.

Cuyler, Margery. *The All-Around Pumpkin Book.* New York: Holt, Rinehart and Winston, 1980.

Friedhoffer, Robert. *How to Haunt a House for Halloween.* New York: Franklin Watts, 1989.

Kessel, Joyce K. *Halloween.* Minneapolis: Carolrhoda Books, 1980.

Patterson, Lillie. *Halloween.* Champaign, Ill.: Garrade Publishing Company, 1963.

Witkowski, Dan. *How to Haunt a House.* New York: Random House, 1994.

UNICEF will provide instructions on how to collect money for poor children. You can get involved by calling 1-800-252-KIDS.

Useful Addresses

Costume Society of America
P.O. Box 73
Earleville, MD 21919-0073

Houdini Historical Center
330 E. College Avenue
Appleton, WI 54911

**International Society for the Study of Ghosts
and Apparitions**
P.O. Box 528124
Chicago, IL 60652-8124

Salem Public Library
370 Essex Street
Salem, MA 01970

Witches Anti-Discrimination Lobby
c/o Hero Press
153 West 80th Street, Suite 1B
New York, NY 10024

World Pumpkin Confederation
14050 Gowanda State Road
Collins, NY 14034

Index

All Hallows Day, 13
All Saints' Day, 13
apples, 13, 27

broomstick, 16-18

cat, 15-18
Celts, 11-13
costume, 5, 8, 12, 24-25, 31, 33-35

devil, 17-18, 22
Druids, 12

ghost, 11, 15, 22-25, 34, 39, 42
graveyard, 23

Houdini, Harry, 24-25

jack-o'-lantern, 5, 8-9, 15, 18, 22, 27, 33, 36

magic, 12, 15-17, 24-25

mask, 12, 25, 33-35

pumpkin, 5, 8, 15, 18, 22, 36, 38

Roman Catholic Church, 13
Romans, 13

sabbat, 17
Salem, Massachusetts, 17
Samhain, 12
skeleton, 22
spirit, 12, 18, 22, 25,

trick or treat, 5, 8, 25, 27-28, 31
turnip, 22, 27

UNICEF, 28, 30

witch, 5, 11, 15-18, 25, 41